Vulture cultu

Story written by Gill Munton
Illustrated by Tim Archbold

Speed Sounds

Consonants   *Ask children to say the sounds.*

f	l	m	n	r	s	v	z	sh	th	ng
ff	ll	mm	nn	rr	ss	ve	zz			nk
ph	le	mb	kn	wr	se		**(se)**			
					c		s			
					ce					

b	c	d	g	h	j	p	qu	t	w	x	y	ch
bb	k	dd	gg		**(g)**	pp		tt	**(wh)**			tch
	ck		**(ge)**		ge							

Each box contains one sound but sometimes more than one grapheme.
*Focus graphemes for this story are **circled**.*

Vowels

Ask children to say the sounds in and out of order.

a	e / ea	i	o	u	ay / a͡e / a / ai / aigh	ee / ea / e / y	igh / i͡e / ie / i / y	ow / o͡e / oa / o / oe

oo / u͡e / ue / ew	oo	ar	or / oor / ore / aw / au	air / are	ir / ur / er	ou / ow	oy / oi	ire	ear	(ure)

Word endings

(ture) / sure	ous / eous / cious / tious	able / ably / ible / ibly	tion

Story Green Words

Ask children to read the words first in Fred Talk and then say the word.

Andean condor   South America   glide   bald   rare

ledge of rock   weigh*   metre*   height*

Ask children to say the syllables and then read the whole word.

vul|ture   na|ture   fea|ture   cap|ture   temp|er|a|ture   ex|tinct

fu|ture   crea|ture   plea|sure

Ask children to read the root first and then the whole word with the suffix.

feather → feathers

* Challenge Words

6

Vocabulary Check

Discuss the meaning (as used in the story) after the children have read each word.

	definition:	sentence:
glide	fly without flapping	They can glide for many hundreds of miles above the mountains.
wing tip	the tip of the wing	From wingtip to wingtip, they can measure more than 3 metres.
bald	no hair	An odd feature of this vulture is its bald head.
rare	unusual	but it is rare for a condor to kill one.
ledge of rock	small ridge on a mountain	They lay the egg on a bare ledge of rock.
temperature	heat	Both parents keep it at the right temperature by sitting on it.
extinct	all gone, died out	In 1973, Andean condors were almost extinct, because too many had been hunted and killed.

Red Words

Ask children to practise reading the words across the rows, down the columns and in and out of order clearly and quickly.

one	some	their	where
they	many	are	were
come	two	of	above
where	there	walk	here
any	through	who	other

Vulture culture

This is a picture of an Andean condor. When it is flying, this huge vulture is one of the most amazing sights in nature. Let's find out some facts about Andean condors and their behaviour.

Where do they live?

These vultures live in the mountain ranges of South America. They can glide for many hundreds of miles above the mountains, looking for food.

What do they look like?

The condor is the largest of the flying birds.
Condors can weigh as much as 13 kilograms.

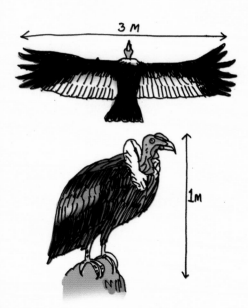

They can measure over
1 metre in height.
From wingtip to wingtip, they can
measure more than 3 metres.

Condors have a mixture of black and white feathers.

The feathers on their bodies are black,

with some white feathers on their necks and wings.

The eyes of a male condor are grey.

The eyes of a female condor are red.

An odd feature of this vulture

is its bald head.

The skin on its head is a dark red.

What do they eat?

They eat animals of all kinds, but it is rare for a condor to kill one.
Flying high above the mountains, a condor can spot
an animal which has died or been killed.
Then it dives down to eat it,
using its beak and claws
to pull the flesh apart.

Now and again, a condor
will capture a baby animal to eat.

How do they breed?

Andean condors start to breed
when they are 6 years old.
Female condors lay their eggs in the summer –
every two years.
They only lay one egg at a time.
They don't make a nest – they lay the egg
on a bare ledge of rock on a cliff or in a cave.
Both parents keep it at the right temperature by sitting on it.

Nearly two months later, a condor chick hatches from the egg.

The chick can't fly until it is about 6 months old,
and its parents have to feed it.

It stays with its parents until it is
at least 1 year old, but then it is ready
for some adventures of its own.

A condor can live for as long
as 50 years.

The future

In 1973, Andean condors were almost extinct, because too many had been hunted and killed.

Nowadays there are many more of them, and the future looks good for these proud creatures. We will have the pleasure of seeing them for many years to come.

Questions to talk about

Ask children to TTYP each question using 'Fastest finger' (FF) or 'Have a think' (HaT).

p.9 (FF) Where in South America do Andean condors live?

p.10 (FF) How many kilograms can they weigh?

p.11 (FF) How can you tell whether a condor is male or female?

p.12 (FF) What animals do condors look for?

p.13 (FF) How many eggs do they lay at a time?

p.14 (FF) How long can condors live for?

p.15 (HaT) Why do you think are there more condors now than in 1973?

Questions to read and answer

(Children complete without your help.)

1. How do Andean condors move around the mountains where they live?

2. What do condors look like?

3. What do condors eat?

4. When do young condors leave their parents?

5. Why do you think condors should be protected from hunters?

Speedy Green Words

Ask children to practise reading the words across the rows, down the columns and in and out of order clearly and quickly.

picture	amazing	largest	behaviour
measure	mixture	parents	adventure
because	picture	amazing	because
animals	again	start	every
time	head	white	year